Life in the Ancient World

Government in the Ancient World

Crabtree Publishing Company

www.crabtreebooks.com

Life in the Ancient World

Contributing authors: Paul Challen, Shipa Mehta-Jones,
   Lynn Peppas, Hazel Richardson
Publishing plan research and development:
   Sean Charlebois, Reagan Miller
   Crabtree Publishing Company
Editors: Kathy Middleton, Adrianna Morganelli
Proofreaders: Kathy Middleton, Marissa Furry
Editorial director: Kathy Middleton
Photo research: Katherine Berti, Crystal Sikkens
Designer and prepress technician: Katherine Berti
Print and production coordinator: Katherine Berti

Cover description:
Many ancient sculptures and carvings were constructed to pay
tribute to government leaders. Examples of this are shown in the
Mesopotamian (top left) and Mayan (bottom right) reliefs, and the
statues of Pharaoh Ramesses II (center), Julius Caesar (top right),
and Alexander the Great (bottom left).

Title page description:
The Forbidden City in Beijing, China, was the ceremonial and
political center of Chinese government for almost five hundred
years. It also served as the home for emperors of the Ming and
Qing dynasties.

Photographs and reproductions:
Bridgeman Art Library: Ashmolean Museum, University of Oxford,
   UK: page 28; Giraudon: page 29
Corbis: Nik Wheeler: page 9 (left); Archivo Inconografico S.A.: p.16
Jeff Jonas: page 10 (left)
Wikimedia commons: page 25 (right); Highshines: page 7 (bottom);
   sailko: page 9 (right); Mamoon Mengal: world66.com: page 10
   (bottom right); Grjatoi: page 10 (top right); BernardM: page 11
   (bottom); Locutus Borg: page 14; Postdlf: page 15 (left);
   Walrasiad: page 17; FA2010: page 18; Simon Burchell: page 19;
   Martin St-Amant: pages 20–21; Ras67: page 24; Shakko: page 25
   (left); Dcoetzee: page 31
All other images by Shutterstock.com

Illustrations:
William Band: pages 26–27, 30

Library and Archives Canada Cataloguing in Publication

Government in the ancient world.

(Life in the ancient world)
Includes index.
Contributing authors: Paul Challen ... [et al.]
Issued also in electronic formats.
ISBN 978-0-7787-1734-8 (bound).--ISBN 978-0-7787-1741-6 (pbk.)

   1. Comparative government--History--To 1500--Juvenile literature.
2. World politics--History--To 1500--Juvenile literature.
I. Challen, Paul, 1967- II. Series: Life in the ancient world (St. Catharines, Ont.)

JF127.G69 2012   j320.3093   C2011-905166-4

Library of Congress Cataloging-in-Publication Data

Government in the ancient world.
   p. cm. -- (Life in the ancient world)
 Includes index.
 ISBN 978-0-7787-1734-8 (reinforced lib. bdg. : alk. paper) -- ISBN 978-0-7787-1741-6
 (pbk. : alk. paper) -- ISBN 978-1-4271-8800-7 (electronic pdf) -- ISBN 978-1-4271-
 9641-5 (electronic html)
 1. Political science--Juvenile literature. 2. Comparative government--Juvenile
 literature. 3. Civilization, Ancient--Juvenile literature. I. Title. II. Series.

JF127.G68 2011
320.309'01--dc23

                                                              2011029258

Crabtree Publishing Company

Printed in Canada/082011/MA20110714

www.crabtreebooks.com   1-800-387-7650

Published in Canada
Crabtree Publishing
616 Welland Ave.
St. Catharines, Ontario
L2M 5V6

Published in the United States
Crabtree Publishing
PMB 59051
350 Fifth Avenue, 59th Floor
New York, New York 10118

Published in the United Kingdom
Crabtree Publishing
Maritime House
Basin Road North, Hove
BN41 1WR

Published in Australia
Crabtree Publishing
3 Charles Street
Coburg North
VIC, 3058

Contents

Government in the Ancient World

Most historians agree that a civilization is a group of people that shares common languages, some form of writing, advanced technology and science, and systems of government and religion. Many ancient cultures were governed, or ruled, by one ruler. Those in power tried to create unity among the peoples of all city-states within their countries.

From Kings to the Birth of Democracy

Government within class systems was important for the prosperity of a civilization. Each culture, from the ancient Chinese to the Vikings, had a caste system, or social hierarchy, whereby people were divided by birth, wealth, and profession. Many ancient civilizations were ruled by the wealthiest families within the city-states. Members at the top of a class system eventually formed senates, such as in ancient Greece and Rome, where men decided how things like taxes were to be spent. These men also often served their city-states as jury members, priests, and judges. Early models of democracy were developed in Greece and Rome, but the Vikings advanced this form of government as the people, rather the rulers, made the laws.

Alexander the Great of Macedon had conquered much of the ancient world by the time he was 20 years old.

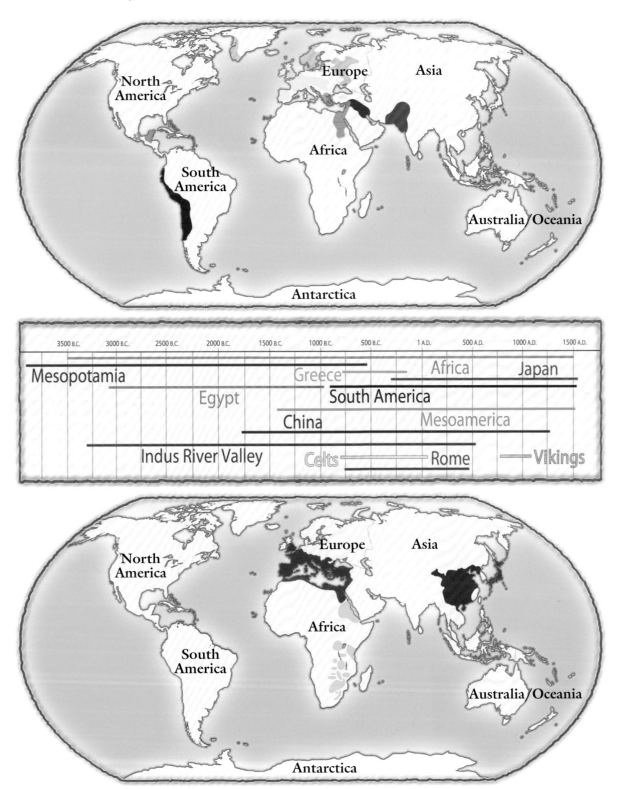

The period described as ancient history is usually defined as the time from first recorded history up to the Early Middle Ages, around 300 A.D. Some of the civilizations in this book begin well after the ancient period but are included because they were dominant early civilizations in their regions. The beginning and ending dates of early civilizations are often subject to debate. For the purposes of this book, the timelines begin with the first significant culture in a civilization and end with the change or disappearance of the civilization. The end was sometimes marked by an event such as invasion by another civilization, or simply by the gradual dispersion of people due to natural phenomena such as famine or earthquakes.

Ancient China

The ancient Chinese people called their emperors "Sons of Heaven," because they believed the leaders were chosen by the gods. Emperors had many wives and many children. When an emperor died, his eldest son usually became emperor. Some Chinese dynasties lasted for hundreds of years. Emperors were China's supreme political, military, and religious leaders.

1766 B.C.–1271 A.D.

Mandate of Heaven

Emperors were expected to act in the best interest of the Chinese people. The Chinese believed that their **ancestors** in heaven brought prosperity and protection to them when an emperor was fair and just. If an emperor acted badly, or was a poor military leader, the heavenly ancestors were thought to show their displeasure by sending earthquakes, floods, and droughts. The people took the natural disasters as a sign to rebel and replace the emperor. The Chinese people called this the Mandate of Heaven.

At the top of ancient Chinese society were the ruling **dynasties**, which included the emperor, his wives and **concubines**, and their immediate families. Members of a dynasty were believed to have been chosen by the spirits of heaven and earth to rule, and were treated like gods by the people. A large army protected every Chinese dynasty. A large group of royal officials, or bureaucrats, ran the government on a day-to-day basis.

Qin Shi Huangdi founded the Qin dynasty and was China's first emperor. The word "China" comes from the name "Qin."

Shang and Zhou Dynasties

China's first known dynasties were founded by the Shang and Zhou peoples. The Shang had large armies with horse-drawn **chariots** and gained control of northern China around 1750 B.C. Shang kings set up large cities and ruled for 600 years. The Zhou people came from the western border of the Shang kingdom and conquered the Shang. Through constant warfare, the Zhou made their kingdom larger, and changed the way China was governed. Zhou kings allowed warriors, or nobles, to own land if they promised to fight for the king in war. This made the nobles more powerful and the king weaker.

Qin Dynasty

In 221 B.C., a ruler named Shi Huangdi came to power. Qin Shi Huangdi moved China's capital to Xianyang and forced nobles to move there with him. By keeping his nobles close to him, Qin Shi Huangdi was able to make sure they did not rebel against him. Qin Shi Huangdi made strict laws and taxed everyone in China. Anyone who opposed his laws was brutally punished. Officials who protested against him were thrown into pits and buried alive. When Qin Shi Huangdi died, rebellions broke out and the Qin dynasty collapsed.

Han Dynasty

The Han dynasty was founded by a government official named Liu Bang in 206 B.C. Over 400 years, the Han emperors expanded China's boundaries and brought peace and prosperity to the people. The Han dynasty organized a civil service to run the **empire**. The civil service was run by government officials who collected taxes, made sure laws were followed, and kept roads and canals in good shape. With people across China following the same laws, a common Chinese culture developed. Today, most Chinese think of themselves as descendants of the Han.

The Sui Dynasty

The Sui dynasty made many changes that strengthened China. Emperor Wendi brought smaller village leaders under his central control and established a census to count people. He also made punishments for lawbreaking the same in every part of the country. China became wealthy during the Sui dynasty and Emperor Wendi reduced the amount of taxes people had to pay. When Wendi's son became emperor, he raised taxes and forced farmers to work on large construction projects, such as the Grand Canal. This made the emperor unpopular and he was **assassinated**, bringing an end to the Sui dynasty.

The Tang Dynasty

The Tang dynasty, which began in 618 A.D., marked a period of great advancement in Chinese culture. This period is referred to as China's Golden Age. Great artistic achievements, such as porcelain making, were developed during the Tang dynasty. Porcelain was made by painting a bright blue dye on clay objects that were not yet dry. A clear glaze was then applied to the clay and it was fired in a kiln, or large oven. Chinese artists began decorating porcelain with elaborate paintings that told the history of the Tang dynasty. Using their powerful armies, China expanded north to what is modern-day Korea, south to modern Vietnam, and west to India during the Tang dynasty. In 906 A.D., the collapse of the Tang dynasty brought disorder to China again.

The Song Dynasty

A military leader who became known as Taizu founded the Song dynasty in 960 A.D. Taizu reformed the Chinese military and government so that people got jobs based on their skill instead of favoritism. The Song built sea-going ships called junks to take Chinese merchants to foreign lands. As trade increased, Chinese merchants became wealthy. Merchants spent money supporting artists, which made the Song era a great period of Chinese art. In the 1100s, most of the ruling Song family was put in prison when the Jin attacked from the north and established the Jin dynasty. A Song son fled south, where he began the Southern Song dynasty in 1127 A.D. Both the Jin and Southern Song were defeated by invading warriors called the Mongols, a people from the north. They became the first foreign rulers of China. Later, when the Manchu invaded, China's traditions continued to survive. Today, almost 100 years after the rule of the last emperor, Puyi, ended in 1912, Chinese civilization continues to influence the world.

Emperors ruled from a palace built in the center of China's capital city.

Empress Wu

China's first empress, Wu Zhao (624–705 A.D.), was one of many wives of Emperor Tang Gaozong. Wu came from a noble family and was known for her intelligence and beauty. She was also ruthless. Wu plotted to replace the emperor's favorite wife and grew very powerful by murdering her enemies. When the emperor died, Wu began ruling China. She built a new capital city, lowered taxes for peasants, and brought in scholars to run the government. Her rule ended when she was forced to step down in 705 A.D.

Ancient Mesopotamia

Mesopotamia is the name given to the region in the Middle East where many different peoples made their homes, including the Sumerians, Akkadians, and Assyrians. Each city-state was independent from the others, with its own leaders, laws, and holidays. The city-state consisted of a central city often protected by a defensive wall, and surrounding towns and villages that depended on the city for leadership, assistance, and protection. Different city-states ruled over the others at various times. Wars and agreements were made between city-states.

Farming Communities

In southern Mesopotamia, the earliest settlements were part of the Ubaid culture. They created small farming villages and towns and built the first temples in Mesopotamia. By 4500 B.C., Ubaid culture had spread to the north, where the farming villages of the Halaf culture already existed. People in the northern villages raised animals, grew grains, hunted wild animals, and gathered plants for food.

The Sumerians

By 3800 B.C., people known as Sumerians ruled southern Mesopotamia. Large settlements in Sumer grew into cities, which eventually became city-states. Some well-known Sumerian city-states were Ur, Lagash, and Uruk. Ur was originally an Ubaid village, but its location close to the Euphrates River made the city one of the most important trading centers by about 2500 B.C.

The Akkadians

The land of Akkad was north of Sumer. The Akkadians conquered Sumer in 2340 B.C., and united all of southern Mesopotamia under one rule. The capital city of the kingdom was Agade. By about 2125 B.C., fighting between city-states led to the collapse of Akkad. Sumerians from the southern city of Ur defeated the Akkadians and ruled southern Mesopotamia again.

The Rise of Babylon

By 2000 B.C., the Amorites, **nomads** from the west, had begun moving into the cities of Sumer. In time, Amorites became kings of most cities in southern Mesopotamia, including Babylon. The Hittites, warriors from the north, conquered Babylon in 1595 B.C. The Hittites left Babylon, and it fell under the rule of the Kassites, a group of nomadic people who had slowly settled throughout southern Mesopotamia. The city of Babylon was ruled by the Kassites until about 1170 B.C.

Sargon the Great led the Akkadian armies against Sumer.

The Birth of Kings

As Sumerian civilization grew, leaders became increasingly more important. Groups of men called Councils of Elders were the first to rule city-states. The Council appointed temporary leaders in times of crises. A leader called an *ensi* was appointed to deal with agricultural problems. A *lugal* was chosen to lead the city's army during times of war. As rivalries worsened among city-states, the power of these leaders grew. By 2800 B.C., the *lugals* had become chief priests, lawmakers, and military commanders.

The Assyrians

Assyria lay between Akkad and the Taurus Mountains. To the south were the more powerful city-states of Mesopotamia. Around 1100 B.C., the Assyrians began to send **military expeditions** west to control important trade routes. By 824 B.C., the Assyrians had conquered all of Mesopotamia, and had built up a large army that used iron weapons and metal armor. To keep control of the lands they conquered, the Assyrian kings ordered the people to relocate to different areas to prevent them from **revolting** against Assyrian rule. Great palaces decorated with carved stone statues and **reliefs** showing military battles were built during the Assyrian empire.

The Babylonians

The Kings of Assyria were not entirely successful in preventing revolts. By 614 B.C., different groups of people, including the Chaldeans in the south and the Medes to the east, had united to fight against Assyrian rule. Together, these groups, who came to be called the Babylonians, established a new Babylonian empire, led by King Nabopolassar. The city of Babylon was rebuilt, but the new empire was weakened by rulers who fought one another for power.

The End of an Age

After the Babylonians defeated Assyria, Mesopotamia was ruled by a series of Babylonian kings who fought one another for power. There were some parts of the empire that were still loyal to Assyria. Babylon's last king was named Nabonidus. The priests of Babylon turned against Nabonidus when he ignored festivals that honored the chief god of the city, Marduk. The priests of Babylon welcomed the invasion of the Persians led by Cyrus the Great in 539 B.C. The Persian army entered the city without a fight, and Babylon became a territory in the Persian empire. By 500 B.C., all of Mesopotamia was controlled by the Persian empire.

(left) The Persian king, Cyrus the Great, took over Babylon.

Hammurabi receives the code of laws from Shamash, the god of Justice.

The Letter of the Law

The Mesopotamian legal system was based on a collection of laws. The laws of Ur-Nammu dates back to around 2100 B.C. It consisted of 57 laws concerning crime, family, inheritance, labor, slaves, and taxes. The best known Mesopotamian collection of laws was the Code of Hammurabi. The law code was written by King Hammurabi, an Amorite king who ruled Babylon from 1792 B.C. to 1750 B.C. The code was very strict, stating the rule of "an eye for an eye, a tooth for a tooth." The 282 laws of Hammurabi's code dealt with family, labor, trade, and property. The laws were carved into eight-foot (three-meter) tall stones that were placed around the kingdom for all to see.

Ancient Indus River Valley

Two of the world's greatest ancient civilizations began in the Indus River Valley, in what is now Pakistan—the Harappans and the Aryans. Historians know more about the Aryan government system and are still learning about the Harappan government.

3300 B.C.–550 A.D.

Historians know each Harappan city had a ruler, who lived in a central palace. They believe that the ruler and his advisors formed a government that determined how a city was built because all Harappan cities were built in the same way.

Aryan Kingdoms

The Aryans lived in *ganas*, which means "collections." A *gana* was made up of several families. Each *gana* had its own territory, ruled by a warrior chief called a *raja*, or king. By 600 B.C., most Aryans had settled by the Ganges River Valley. This area was divided into sixteen kingdoms, each ruled by a *raja*. The most powerful kingdom was Magadha.

Invasions and Conquerors

India's ancient history is one of invasion and adaptation. The Aryans were the first invaders to leave their mark. In 500 B.C., Aryan India was invaded by the Persians who conquered the Indus River Valley. The Persian rulers were then conquered by the Greeks in 327 B.C., led by Macedonian general, Alexander the Great. Alexander returned to Greece but left men behind to look after trade routes he established.

The Mauryan Age

After Alexander left, a *raja* named Chandragupta Maurya killed the *raja* of Magadha and made himself emperor in 321 B.C. Chandragupta Maurya was not afraid to kill those who went against his ideas. By the end of his reign, Chandragupta Maurya's territory extended from the Ganges and Indus rivers to most of Afghanistan. The capital of his empire, Pataliputra, had elaborate temples, a university, a library, and public parks. Chandragupta Maurya and the emperors who followed him established a period of rule called the Mauryan Empire.

Elephants were used in battle by many dynasties in ancient India.

Mohenjo-daro

A priest or king figure excavated from the ancient Harappan city of Mohenjo-daro, on the bank of the Indus River

The Reign of Asoka

Chandragupta's grandson, Asoka, was one of India's most famous rulers. In 260 B.C., Asoka sent his army to conquer the native peoples of southern India. The slaughter that followed horrified Asoka. He began to study the new Indian religion of **Buddhism**, which said killing is wrong and that all men are equal and deserve respect. He was so impressed with Buddhist ideas that he made Buddhism the official religion of his kingdom. Asoka ordered thousands of stone pillars and *stupas*, or monuments whose domed shape is said to represent the Buddha, to be raised across India. The *stupas* were carved to show laws on how to behave. These laws were known as *dharma*.

End of an Empire

When the ruler of the Mauryans was assassinated in 185 B.C., the empire broke apart. India then split into a number of smaller kingdoms that were often invaded by other peoples such as the Greeks, and the Persians. In 320 A.D., another strong ruler named Chandra Gupta brought India under his control. Chandra Gupta was not related to Chandragupta Maurya. His empire was called the Gupta empire. The Gupta empire spread south and over hundreds of years made great advances in art, science, and literature. The empire fell apart in 550 A.D. after the Huns, invaders from western China, took over parts of the empire.

After the Gupta empire, India returned to being a nation of city-states ruled by *rajas*. In the south, the **indigenous** peoples, called the Dravidians, lived in kingdoms divided from the north by forests and mountains that were difficult for armies to cross. In 1000 A.D., Arabs conquered the city-states in the north. The Arabs intoduced their religion, **Islam**, and over time, Muslim rulers established new empires called the Delhi Sultanate and the Moghul dynasty. The Moghul dynasty ruled northern India from the 1500s until the early 1800s, expanding with each ruler. After 1858, India came under British **colonial** rule, and the south and north were once again united.

This monument in Sanchi, called the Great Stupa, was one of thousands of stupas erected by the emperor Asoka after his conversion to Buddhism. This stupa held relics, or objects associated with a saint or matyr, of the Buddha.

Did Aryans Destroy Harappan Cities?

The Rig-Veda is a collection of 1,000 hymns composed between 1500 B.C. and 800 B.C. Some of these hymns describe Aryan warriors destroying large cities and killing the dark-skinned, curly haired people who lived there. Some archaeologists think these stories describe the Aryans attacking the Harappans. Others believe the stories are exaggerations.

Ancient Greece

800 B.C.–146 B.C.

The Greeks gave the world democracy, a form of government born in Athens, and belief in the worth of individual people. The earliest peoples of Greece were the Minoans and the Mycenaeans. Around 800 B.C., independent city-states, such as Athens and Sparta, rose up across the Greek mainland. Greek city-states were strong when they were united, but when they battled each other, they became vulnerable to outsiders.

Minoans and Mycenaeans

The Minoans built the first great Greek civilization on the island of Crete in the Mediterranean Sea between 2200 B.C. and 1400 B.C. Around 1580 B.C., a war-like people settled in a coastal city in the southern Peloponnese called Mycenae. The Mycenaneans ruled Greece for 400 years before their civilization collapsed. The end of the Mycenanean civilization plunged Greece into a period called the Dark Ages, which lasted until 800 B.C.

From Tyranny to Democracy

Around 800 B.C., the Greek people began founding a number of small, independent city-states. Each city-state, or *polis*, controlled the villages and farmland around it and had its own laws, government, and system of money. At first, all city-states were ruled by a *basileus*, or king. Most kings were overthrown by the people and replaced with oligarchies.

Oligarchies were governments where only a few wealthy citizens ruled. In some city-states, tyrants came to power by overthrowing the kings or oligarchies. Tyrants were men who held onto power by military force and fear. Some tyrants ruled for years, but over time people began to favor oligarchy or democracy.

Sparta

The city-state of Sparta was founded in 950 B.C. and organized as a military camp. Sparta was a city-state that was almost constantly at war or preparing for war. Over time, Sparta conquered almost all the surrounding lands in the Peloponnese, using the land for farming and forcing the conquered people into slavery. Spartans were heavily outnumbered by their slaves and servants and so needed to rule by fear. Slaves in Sparta were called helots and were forced to do heavy work while Spartan men dedicated themselves to war. Sparta was ruled by an oligarchy of two military generals. The generals made all the decisions and ordinary citizens had no power.

Athens

By the mid-400s B.C., Athens had grown into the most powerful city-state in Greece. Athens created a new form of government based on the rule of the people. It was called democracy, from the Greek word *demos*, meaning "the people." Every male citizen got a vote when it came to electing officials to run the city and make laws, but women and slaves were not allowed to vote. The main governing body was the assembly of all citizens, or *ecclesia*, which gathered 40 times a year on a hillside. In 508 B.C., the Athenian leader Cleisthenes guaranteed that free adult male citizens were automatically members of the *ecclesia*. In times of war, ten military generals called *strategoi* made decisions about defending the city.

Pericles was a general elected by the Athenian people fourteen times. Pericles undertook many large building projects, such as the Acropolis.

Democracy in Action

The *ecclesia* in Athens met in a hillside amphitheater that seated 18,000 people. All citizens could make a speech and vote at the *ecclesia*. A smaller group of people, called the *boule*, met daily to decide what important business the *ecclesia* would discuss and vote on. The *boule* was made up of 500 citizens who were chosen randomly. Laws that were passed by the *ecclesia* were upheld by the courts. Athenian courts had no judges or lawyers. An official kept order while a person accused of a crime defended himself. A jury of between 200 and 2,500 citizens was drawn from names in a bowl. The jury determined whether a person was guilty or not guilty. During a trial, jurors were given two ballots to use to cast a vote. A ballot with a hollow post, or center, meant guilty and one with a solid post meant not-guilty.

Waging War

Fighting in a war was the supreme test of a Greek man. A city-state prospered if it had a strong navy to protect it from invaders such as the Persians, and from pirates of the Aegean Sea who preyed on its trading ships. In Athens, the citizens voted for people to fill all important jobs. Military generals were elected and every citizen could be called on to fight. One method of voting was to drop a colored stone into a vase. Whoever had the most stones won the vote. At age eighteen, Athenian men from wealthy families went for two years of training for war. Open spaces around the *gymnasia*, or schools for physical education, were used to train the Athenian cavalry and army.

The Persian Wars

By 500 B.C., the kingdom of Persia to the east of Greece had grown powerful. The Persians repeatedly attacked and conquered Greek colonies in Asia Minor and North Africa. In 490 B.C., the Persian ruler Darius I tried to attack the city of Athens. The two armies fought a battle near the village of Marathon, and the Athenians won. In 480 B.C., the Persians attacked again. Sparta's army led an **alliance** of 31 city-states against the invading Persians. The Persian navy was lured into a narrow channel off the island of Salamis in the Aegean Sea where their ships got trapped. The Greek ships were smaller and fitted with rams, which crushed their enemy's hulls. The Greek ships destroyed the Persian navy and the Persian army fled. The Persians never returned.

The Peloponnesian War

After the Persian Wars, Athens organized another alliance of city-states, called the Delian League, to protect Greece from future Persian attacks. Since all the members of the alliance had to send **tribute** to Athens, the Athenians became very powerful. Sparta resented Athenian power and created an alliance of city-states to oppose Athens. In 459 B.C., Sparta and its allies defeated Athens in the first Peloponnesian War. Twenty-eight years later, the strong navy of Athens attacked Corinth, one of Sparta's allies. In response, Sparta began the second Peloponnesian War, which lasted until 404 B.C. Sparta eventually won when it built a navy to oppose Athens at sea. Sparta replaced Athenian democracy with an oligarchy.

Alexander the Great

By 338 B.C., King Philip of Macedon to the north of Greece had conquered Athens, Sparta, and most other Greek city-states. At age 20, his son Alexander, who became known as Alexander the Great, expanded Philip's kingdom to include Egypt, India, and Persia.

Alexander the Great

Alexander thought highly of the Greek way of life. He settled Greeks in the conquered cities as a way to strengthen his control. The Macedonian conquest changed the Greek way of life, but it also preserved and spread Greek culture. This period in history is known as the Hellenistic Age.

In about 350 B.C., Rome emerged as a power on the neighboring peninsula of Italy. Over time, the powerful army of Rome defeated its neighbors. By 146 B.C., all of ancient Greece was under Roman rule.

Foot soldiers called **hoplites** *were usually wealthy citizens. Only the wealthy could supply their own weapons and armor.*

Ancient Egypt

Ancient Egypt was ruled by a series of kings, or pharaohs, who were thought to be the representatives of the gods on Earth. The power to rule was kept in the family, or dynasty. A pharaoh usually passed his position on to his son, who passed it on to the next generation. From about 2650 B.C. to 1500 B.C., pharaohs were buried in enormous stone tombs called pyramids **when they died. Each pyramid took many years and thousands of workers to build. Many still stand today.**

Before the Old Kingdom

The period of time before the Old Kingdom is called the Pre-Dynastic Period (3100 B.C. to 2686 B.C.). During this time, nomadic hunters began to settle permanently on the banks of the Nile. They grew crops and developed an early form of writing. These early Egyptians buried their kings under large flat slabs of dried mud called mastabas, or benches.

Two Kingdoms

Early Egypt was divided into two kingdoms, Upper Egypt and Lower Egypt. Pharaohs in Upper Egypt wore white crowns and those in Lower Egypt wore red crowns. Around 3100 B.C., a pharaoh named Narmer from Upper Egypt united the two kingdoms. Historians believe that Narmer was also known as Menes, since pharaohs often had several names. Narmer and those who followed his rule in the first and second dynasties held power for about 400 years.

The Old Kingdom (2700 B.C. to 2200 B.C.)

Pharaohs became very powerful during the Old Kingdom. Pharaohs were often brave warriors who commanded the army. Strong military leadership was important to Egyptians since their kingdoms were sometimes attacked by their neighbors. Pharaohs also directed trade with other nations, made laws, and punished those who broke them. Punishments included fines, hard labor, beatings, and even death. Royal advisors called *viziers* and low-level officials from all over Egypt helped the pharaoh with his daily work of governing.

The Middle Kingdom (2200 B.C. to 1800 B.C.)

The pharaoh decided which family member would succeed him after his death. Pharaoh Pepi II ruled for over 90 years but did not name an heir before he died. Many kings fought to claim control of Egypt after his death. This time of war is called the First Intermediate Period. By 2040 B.C., princes from the city of Thebes in Upper Egypt had gained control. This era is known as the Middle Kingdom. Egypt built a strong army to conquer the neighboring lands of Nubia and Kush in the south. At first, Egyptians used only shields, swords, and spears. By the 13th dynasty, when a people called the Hyksos defeated Egypt, Egyptians had learned how to use horses and chariots in battle. Pharaohs hired foreign soldiers, called mercenaries, to help in battle. The Hyksos victory marked the end of the Middle Kingdom.

The Narmer Palette is a slab of stone that marks the victory of the Pharaoh Narmer. Narmer united the two kingdoms of Upper and Lower Egypt after a great battle.

The New Kingdom (1600 B.C. to 1100 B.C.)

During the New Kingdom, Egypt reached the height of its power. The New Kingdom is best known for three pharaohs: Hatshepsut, Akhenaton, and Ramses II.

Amenhotep IV was a pharaoh who believed that the priests who ran the temples had been given too much religious power by previous pharaohs. To change this, he ordered Egyptians to follow only one god, Aten, instead of Amun-Re, the chief god of all Egypt. He also changed his name to Akhenaton which meant "agreeable to Aten." Akhenaton replaced all symbols of Amun-Re with Aten on monuments. He also declared everyone should worship him as Aten's representative. Unpopular when he died, his successor, Tutenkhamen, restored Amun-Re.

Pharaoh Ramses II was another New Kingdom ruler who considered himself a great warrior. Ramses II tried to win back lands lost during wars in Akhenaton's reign. After Ramses II, assaults on Egypt became far more common. Ramses III defended Egypt against attackers from the Mediterranean called the "Sea People." Although Egypt won the battles, it was seriously weakened. It could no longer conquer other lands, nor fend off invaders.

Invasion

Egypt was next ruled by the family of a Libyan conqueror named Sheshonk, followed by the Nubians, who ruled a kingdom to the south. Egypt's next invader came from Assyria, where the modern country of Iraq is located. After capturing Egypt, the Assyrians left an Egyptian prince named Psammetichus to rule Egypt for them. He invited other foreigners to settle in Egypt. In 525 B.C., invaders from Persia, or modern Iran, captured Egypt. Alexander the Great of Macedon entered Egypt with his army in 332 B.C., forcing the Persians from Egypt. The Egyptians treated him as a hero.

Alexander moved Egypt's capital to a new city by the Mediterranean Sea and named it Alexandria. After his death, a dynasty of kings, all named Ptolemy, ruled from Alexandria. They made Greek the official language of Egypt. Greek citizens arrived in Egypt and took the most important jobs. The Egyptian religion was honored, however, and temples continued to be built for their gods.

The Final Blow

By 200 B.C., the Roman Empire had begun to conquer the ancient peoples of the Mediterranean. By 50 B.C., Rome was strong enough to force Egypt to do as it asked without invading. Julius Caesar, the Emperor of Rome, made Egypt's young queen Cleopatra his mistress. When Caesar died, two Roman leaders, Octavian and Marc Antony, competed to take control of Rome. Cleopatra became Marc Antony's mistress. When Cleopatra and Marc Antony were defeated in battle by Octavian's army, they committed suicide. Cleopatra was ancient Egypt's last ruler. With her death, one of the greatest civilizations of the ancient world had come to an end. Octavian celebrated his conquest by changing his name to Augustus and Egypt became part of the Roman Empire.

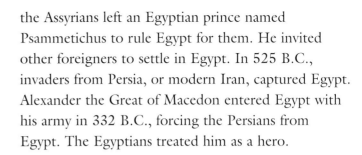

Hatshepsut

Hatshepsut was the main wife of Thutmose II. After he died without an heir, she wore the clothing of kings and a false beard to become pharaoh. Hatshepsut was very successful and ruled for twenty years. She strengthened the navy and sent trade missions to the African coast.

The Temple of Karnak at Luxor was built over a period of several centuries. It was dedicated to the god Amun-Re, the chief god of Egypt and the protector of the pharaohs.

15

Ancient Africa

Many cultures co-existed in ancient Africa. The Nubians, Aksumites, and the peoples of Great Zimbabwe and the western African civilizations developed wealthy trading societies ruled by kings, queens, or pharaohs. They inherited the throne by being born into the royal family. Local chiefs and members of the ruler's family made up the government and helped the ruler make laws, collect taxes, and control trade. Some societies did not have a ruler, but were organized by family groups, or clans.

Kings and Clans

Ancient African cultures were led by the most powerful and wealthy people, who were the kings, queens, pharaohs, and nobles. They controlled land and trade. Some ancient African societies were led by a village elder, priest, or the head of a powerful clan. Sometimes the most important person was the person who owned the most cattle.

Pharaohs of Egypt

The ruler, or king, in ancient Egypt was called a pharaoh. The ancient Egyptians believed that each pharaoh was a god who had descended from the sun god Amun-Ra. After each pharaoh died, his body was mummified to prevent decay, then wrapped in bandages and placed in a decorated coffin called a sarcophagus.

Nubian Pharaohs

To the south of ancient Egypt lay the land of the Nubian people. The Egyptians called this land Kush. The Nubians developed a great civilization that lasted from 2500 B.C. until 300 A.D. Egypt invaded Kush in 1550 B.C. and ruled the Nubians for 450 years. After Egyptian rule ended, the Nubians began to build up their armies and wealth. By 757 B.C., they were so strong that they invaded and conquered Egypt. For the next 100 years, Nubians ruled Egypt. After the Nubians left Egypt, their kings continued to act like pharaohs but, unlike in Egypt, many of the rulers were women. The ruler was chosen from the royal family, usually by the mother of the king or queen. The most famous Nubian female pharaoh was Amanirenas, who led her army against invaders from Rome, a civilization that arose in what is Italy today. Amanirenas lost an eye in battle but still fought to victory.

Aksumite King of Kings

Around 500 B.C., a group of people migrated from Arabia across the Red Sea to Africa. The migrants intermarried with people already living there. These people eventually became the Aksumite civilization. The Aksumite people called their king *negusa nagast*, which means "king of kings." Aksumite kings were strong rulers who expanded the kingdom and its trade routes. The Aksumites traded with the ancient Greeks. King Zoskales was a strong Aksumite ruler who was often described in ancient Greek writings as a king who boldly demanded trade treaties, or agreements, with ancient Rome and India.

The pharaohs of Kush wore a crown with a double cobra on the front to show they controlled both Egypt and Nubia.

Ghana's Warrior Kings

In 600 A.D., in an area of western Africa between present-day Mauritania and Mali, the empire of Ghana developed into one of the most powerful African kingdoms. Led by the Soninke people, ancient Ghana expanded its land and wealth by conquering many neighboring peoples with its strong army. Ancient Ghana had a supreme ruler, known as the ghana, or "warrior king." The king became very wealthy by charging traders a tax, payable in gold, on the goods that traveled through his land. A huge army enforced the king's rule. In ancient Ghana, kingship passed through the female side of the family. The throne was inherited by the son of the old king's sister.

Mali's Mansas

The Mali civilization was developed by the Mandinke people, who controlled the land south of the kingdom of Ghana. Between 1230 and 1430, the Mandinke people took over surrounding communities, eventually developing a large civilization called the kingdom of Mali. Mali controlled the empire of Ghana's old territory and surrounding land, in what are now in the present-day countries of Senegal, Mauritania, Guinea, and Mali. The kings of ancient Mali were called Mansa, an Arabic word meaning sultan, or king. Mali's most famous Mansa was Sundiata, the Lion King. During his reign, Sundiata conquered neighboring territories, built libraries and universities, and introduced cotton growing and weaving to his nation.

Songhai Generals

The Songhai kingdom, in what is today northwest Nigeria and western Sudan, began around 800 A.D. The Songhai kingdom became the largest empire in Africa, with several thousand cultures under its control. Sonni Ali Ber, the first Songhai king, was famous for expanding the Mali territory of Songhai into a strong empire. His army captured the Mali city-state of Timbuktu, an important trading post and learning center. Sonni Ali Ber was not a popular ruler because he did not think education was important. After his death in 1492, the new king appointed scholars from Timbuktu to the government and made learning important to the Songhai people.

Benin

In the forests of western Africa, people lived in small villages ruled by chiefs. Between 1000 and 1500 A.D., some of the village chiefs made alliances with each other and formed states. The largest state was Benin, in what is now southern Nigeria. Its capital was Edo, now Benin City. Benin rulers and nobles lived in the cities. They wore brass medallions to show their ranks.

Ancient Zimbabwe

Ancestors of the Bantu-speaking people, today known as the Shona, settled on the Zimbabwe Plateau around 200 A.D. Using granite from the plateau, they built many cities, including a religious and political center that became known as Great Zimbabwe. This city, which was home to about 18,000 people, featured a hilltop palace and a high stone walled enclosure.

Europeans Colonize Africa

From the 1500s through the 1800s, England, Germany, Portugal, Italy, France, and Holland seized most of Africa and divided it among themselves. The European colonizers often plundered Africa's natural resources and destroyed many African monuments and historical treasures. Africans resisted enslavement and European colonization, sometimes quietly and sometimes through armed struggle. Many of these struggles, in which colonial governments and ways of life were toppled and replaced with African ones, continued until the late 1900s.

Mansa Musa, a wealthy and generous Mali ruler, was depicted on a European map from 1375 that showed his territory.

Ancient Mesoamerica

Mesoamericans did not have a single government. The civilizations that developed in the region between North and South America—the Olmec, Maya, and Aztec—each had their own communities, or city-states. A city-state had a ruler, and each ruler was treated like a god. Sometimes city-states fought other city-states and created empires. Some city-states joined together in alliances to protect themselves from conquerors.

Rulers

Usually, a king or chief priest was the most important figure in society. For the Aztecs, an even more powerful ruler, called an emperor, was required to govern the three city-states of Tenochtitlán, Texcoco, and Tlacopan.

In Mesoamerican society, the chief priest was also the king. Most often, the king inherited the position from a family member, usually on his father's side. The king governed his own city-state. In a few royal families, a woman filled the role of ruler when the king was unable. Some royal and noble women also took part in ritual sacrifices of humans, and worked as healers, midwives, and priestesses. The people believed the king was god-like and could speak directly to the gods.

Mesoamericans at War

War occurred constantly in Mesoamerica. City-states sometimes fought over territory but more often, Mesoamericans fought each other to gain riches and to capture prisoners. Some captured warriors were used as slaves. Leaders who were captured were tortured and sacrificed to please the gods. The number of prisoners taken captive by a victorious warrior proved how powerful he was, and increased his fortune in the army.

Olmec City-States

The Olmecs created the first civilization in Mesoamerica. The Olmecs were nomadic hunters who settled into farming communities in the lowland areas near the Gulf of Mexico and the central valley highlands around 1200 B.C. The Olmec people built city-states with grand pyramid-shaped temples in the center that were used for religious ceremonies. They were ruled by governors, called Ku, and kings, called Tu. Olmec rulers lived in the cities while everyone else lived outside the city. Olmec rulers also served as religious leaders and grew very powerful over the city-states and the surrounding area.

Maya City-States

The Maya civilization reached its peak between 250 and 900 A.D. The Maya built a kingdom of at least 5 city-states. Each city-state was made up of a large urban center and the surrounding farming communities. The size of a Maya city-state was usually about the distance a person could walk in a day. The urban center had pyramids, temples, and great monuments which were lined up with the sun, moon, and stars.

In this sculpture from a temple, a Maya king is presented with slaves.

Maya city-states were not united with each other. The city-states of Tikal and Calakmul were more powerful than the others and controlled smaller city-states. City-states defeated in war had to pay tribute to their conquerors with precious items such as quetzal feathers, cocoa beans, and fine cloth. Quetzal feathers come from a tropical bird and were worn on the headdresses of royals. Cocoa beans were used to make chocolate, which was highly prized by ancient Mesoamericans.

Maya Rulers

A king ruled each Maya city-state. The king's power was handed down to first-born boys on the father's side. The Maya believed a king had special powers to communicate with the gods. Maya kings wore elaborate clothing and headdresses representing animals to identify them as gods. Kings negotiated trading alliances, maintained the business of the state, and organized construction projects. The king planned military battles to expand and defend a city's territory and capture prisoners for sacrifice to the gods.

The Aztec

The Aztec were a warrior-like group that settled on a snake-inhabited island in the Valley of Mexico's Lake Texcoco in the early 1100s A.D. The neighboring peoples hoped the rattlesnakes on the island would force the Aztec to leave, but the Aztecs were determined to stay and developed new recipes for rattlesnake meat. For nearly 400 years, the Aztec ruled the region from their mighty city of Tenochtitlán, which they built on the island. They were destroyed by Spanish soldiers who arrived in Tenochtitlán in the early 1500s.

Aztec Empire: The Triple Alliance

The Aztec empire was tied together through royal and noble marriages. Aztec nobles married their sons and daughters to family members to create powerful ruling families. Children of royalty in conquered states were all educated at Tenochtitlán, so royal children all knew one another. As Tenochtitlán grew and prospered, the citizens of the nearby city of Tepanec began to fear that the Aztec would conquer them. To prevent this, they killed the Aztec king. Tlacaelel, a brutal but brilliant Aztec military commander, defeated the Tepanec people in retaliation. His uncle, Itzcoatl, also called the Obsidian Serpent, then made Tenochtitlán an ally with the cities of Texcoco and Tlacopan. This Triple Alliance of Aztec cities began conquering smaller, surrounding city-states until it controlled most of what is now central Mexico.

Death of Motecuhzoma

Spanish explorer Hernán Cortés marched to Tenochtitlán and met Aztec emperor Motecuhzoma on November 8, 1519. Motecuhzoma thought Cortés was the god Quetzalcoatl, whom legend said would one day return, and invited the Spanish leader and his army to rest at his palace. Cortés and his men were uneasy about staying there, and decided to hold Motecuhzoma hostage so the Aztecs would not harm them.

When Cortés was called away on a military matter, he took 100 soldiers with him and left the rest at Motecuhzoma's palace. Cortés returned to find his men in trouble and forced Motecuhzoma to talk the Aztecs out of fighting. The Aztecs threw rocks at Motecuhzoma. When he died a few days later, the Spanish said the rocks thrown by the Aztecs had killed the ruler, but the Aztecs maintained that Motecuhzoma was strangled by the Spanish. The cause of Motecuhzoma's death remains a mystery today.

Pacal of Palenque

The best known Maya king was Lord Pacal who lived in the city of Palenque between 603 A.D. and 683 A.D. Palenque flourished under the rule of Pacal. Great palaces were built and decorated with **stucco** paintings that depicted the rulers and their families.

The hairstyle of this stucco head of Pacal looks like maize, or corn, leaves to connect him with the maize god.

Ancient South America

Ancient South American civilizations were ruled by high priests or kings. Most people were farmers or artisans who supported the rulers and their families by giving them food and items they produced. Few details are known about the way the earliest South American societies were run. Historians know most about Inca government from the writings of Spanish conquistadors.

The Sapa Inca

The ruler, or emperor of the Incas, was called the Sapa Inca. He performed religious ceremonies on special occasions, such as the first plowing of the fields in spring. The Sapa Inca was believed to be descended from the sun god, Inti, and was worshiped by his people as a god. Traditionally, the Sapa Inca married his eldest sister, who became known as the Coya. The Sapa Inca also had many other wives. If the Sapa Inca had a son with the Coya, the child became heir to the throne. If the Sapa Inca did not have a son with the Coya, he chose one of his other sons to be the next emperor.

Pachacuti expanded the Inca empire into Ecuador, Bolivia, and Chile.

Life of the Sapa Inca

Each Sapa Inca had a palace built for him in the capital city, Cuzco. When a Sapa Inca traveled, servants carried him on a golden litter lined with colorful feathers. Women and children walked ahead of him, sweeping the ground, playing music, and strewing flowers. His face was hidden by fabric because his appearance was thought to be too powerful for humans to see. When a Sapa Inca died, his body was mummified and kept in his palace. During religious festivals, the body was paraded through the streets of Cuzco.

The Greatest Emperor

At first, the Incas controlled only the land around their capital, Cuzco. In 1438, Cuzco was attacked by the Chanca, a neighboring people. The Sapa Inca fled the city, but his son, Yupanqui, led the army to defeat the Chancas. Yupanqui changed his name to Pachacuti, meaning "he who changed the world," and ruled the Incas for 30 years.

Land of Four Parts

By 1480, millions of people lived within the Inca empire. The empire was so large that it was divided into four regions. Close male relatives of the Sapa Inca were made lords of each region. The lords made up a council that advised the Sapa Inca on important matters.

Curacas, the Local Lords

The Sapa Inca controlled all of the land in the empire. Plots of land were given to groups of families called *allyus*. The families of an *allyu* worked together to farm the land. The empire's four regions were divided into many **provinces**. Each province was run by a governor, who was a male member of the Sapa Inca's family. The governor appointed **administrators**, or *curacas*, to run the households in his province. *Curacas* were in charge of the land each household was given to farm, and made sure taxes were paid. *Curacas* supervised many households. Leaders of peoples who were conquered by the Incas were often made *curacas*. *Curacas* could be men or women.

Inca Taxes

Each Inca community was divided into three parts. Harvests from one part were distributed among the people so that everyone was fed. Crops from the other two portions of farmland were given to nobles and administrators. Llama and alpaca herds were divided among the people in the same way. Every family received all the food, housing, and wool it needed. If a crop failed, the people were given food from the government's supply.

As payment, people had to pay taxes to the government in the form of either labor or goods. Each year, men worked for a set number of days under a system of public service called *mita*. Some panned for gold in streams, while others built **irrigation** canals, roads, and temples. Artisans were required to make a certain amount of goods, such as pottery and jewelry, for their Inca rulers each year. Women wove cloth in their homes and sent the finest textiles to the ruling class as tax payment.

Crime and Punishment

Theft was rare in the Inca empire, as people were given what they needed by the government. When they did occur, crimes were harshly punished. Thieves had their hands and feet cut off. Each day they were carried to the city gates and left to beg for food. Murderers were thrown to their deaths off cliffs.

Conquered Peoples

The Incas developed their large empire by taking over land that was lived on by other peoples. Some peoples were happy to join the Inca empire, because they knew they would be given food and housing in return for their labor. Those unwilling to join the Inca empire were conquered anyway, but were allowed to keep some of their customs as well as languages. Conquered peoples were taught Inca farming and weaving techniques, and paid taxes to the emperor as the Incas did.

End of the Empire

The Incas established a mighty empire that brought over ten million people under one rule. In 1531, hundreds of gold-seeking Spanish landed in the north of the empire. The conquistadors, who had already wiped out the native civilizations of Mexico, soon also destroyed the Inca civilization. Especially after being weakened by smallpox, the Incas, with their quilted cotton armor and spears, were no match for the Spanish, who had metal armor, guns, and horses. In 1572, the spanish killed the last Inca leader, Tupac Amaru.

The Incas' Long Ears

Earplugs were pieces of metal, such as gold, or pieces of shell, that men pushed through their earlobes like earrings. This made their earlobes longer. Moche and Inca men wore earplugs to show their status in society. When Spanish explorers came to Peru, the custom was still practiced. The Spanish called Inca noblemen "long ears" because of this custom.

This walled fortress outside Cuzco is made of large polished stones. The Inca cut the stones to fit together so the walls did not need mortar.

Ancient Rome

Rome's ideal location and climate made it attractive to waves of settlers who ruled for a time, were defeated, and replaced by newcomers. Each group influenced the next through the religion, language, or culture it left behind. The Romans conquered people and lands by building and keeping a strong, well-trained army. As Rome gained power, it became an unstoppable force.

753 B.C.–476 A.D.

Etruscan Kings

Around 800 B.C., a group of people called the Etruscans moved to the area around Rome. They came from Etruria, in northern Italy. The Etruscans expanded their territory, but by 350 B.C. the Etruscans began to lose power to the Romans. Eventually, the Romans drove the Etruscans back to Etruria.

Roman Republic (509-31 B.C.)

Freed from Etruscan rule, the Romans formed a **republic** in which many people held power, rather than being ruled by one king. The republic lasted for hundreds of years. During this time, all male citizens of Rome were allowed to vote. In the early years of the republic, only members of Rome's wealthy families were elected as magistrates, or government officials.

Magistrates held power for one year and helped make laws. Two chief magistrates, called consuls, were also elected each year. They served as judges, chief priests, and proposers of law. All magistrates had to agree on decisions. Romans wanted to keep the republic free of leaders who acted like kings. In the early days of the republic, Rome's rules, or laws, were published on bronze plates called the twelve tablets. The tablets contained laws on land ownership, inheritance, trespassing, contracts and eventually criminal laws and the punishments for crimes.

Senate and the Forum

In later years, Rome's government included senators and two assemblies. Senators were wealthy nobles who gave advice. The senate had control over whether tax money would be spent on war or for public works such as buildings and roads. Senate chambers, where the senate met, law courts, and public meeting places were arranged around the forum. The forum was like a town square with many buildings, including temples, speakers' platforms, and libraries. During the republic, Rome expanded its territory, and added new provinces by going to war with neighboring lands. Rome conquered all of Italy and parts of western Europe, including areas of modern Spain, France, and Africa.

The Army

Rome had an army of about 30 legions. Each legion had from 5,000 to 8,000 men. The legions were divided into different groups. This army of 450,000 men policed an amazing 1,700,000 square miles (4,400,000 square kilometers). Ordinary foot soldiers were called legionaries and a group of soldiers on horseback was called a cavalry. Just above the rank of legionaries were veterinarians, doctors, and musicians. Legionaries marched 20 miles (32 km) a day in thick leather jackets or, if they had money, in armor made from sheet iron and wire. They carried a shield, food, and a javelin or sword. Soldiers stayed in the army for 25 years, if they survived that long. They were given land after their 25 years of service.

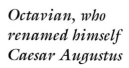

Octavian, who renamed himself Caesar Augustus

The End of the Republic

The Roman republic survived through a civil war and a number of dictators who murdered their opponents to gain wealth and land. The republic finally ended in 44 B.C. when a group of senators stabbed and killed Gaius Julius Caesar. Julius Caesar was a Roman army general and consul who became a dictator and ignored the rules and laws of the republic. After Caesar's death, several generals fought each other for power. Rome's citizens rebelled and another civil war broke out.

The Early Empire (31 B.C.–235 A.D.)

The war and unrest continued until Julius Caesar's friend and co-consul Mark Antony made a deal to rule the Roman empire with Caesar's adopted son Gaius Julius Caesar Octavianus, called Octavian. Until 31 B.C., they ruled different parts of the empire. Octavian then defeated Antony and with the senate's approval ruled the empire alone. Octavian took the name Caesar to honor his adopted father. He is also known as the emperor Augustus. Under Augustus, Romans saw the beginning of a century of peace and stability, called the Pax Romana.

After Augustus' death, he was replaced by a series of 90 emperors over 500 years. Some of those emperors were clever leaders. During Claudius's reign (41 A.D. to 54 A.D.), the empire expanded to include Britain. Claudius was also a writer and historian. His wife poisoned him so her son Nero could become emperor. Trajan (98 A.D. to 117 A.D.) was born in Spain and was the first emperor to come from Rome's provinces. Trajan set up a program to give money to poor children, called the alimenta. He built roads, bridges, and **aqueducts** in the Roman provinces. During Trajan's reign, the Roman army expanded the empire to its furthest reaches. Some emperors were poor leaders who spent time plotting the deaths of rivals, including family members. Emperors Caligula and Caracalla ordered the murder of so many people during their reigns that they were thought to be insane. Both were assassinated.

Many of Rome's rulers were **despots**, who used Rome's senate to pass laws that benefitted only the emperor's family and other patricians' families. Rome's rulers offered entertainment in the arenas, such as bloody gladiatorial competitions, to distract Rome's unemployed and unhappy citizens. With poor and weak rulers, Romans lost faith in their government and empire.

Between 200 A.D. and 300 A.D., no single Roman emperor lived long enough to command the army and successfully push back the barbarians, a group of people who fought for control of Rome's territories. The empire had 23 rulers in 100 years, only one of whom died of natural causes.

Decline of the Empire (235 A.D.–476 A.D.)

During the reign of Hadrian (117 A.D. to 136 A.D.), Rome's territory began to shrink. Hadrian constructed walls along Rome's farthest borders to keep out invaders. Rome's mighty army began to lose battles to barbarian invaders in some of its provinces. Under Emperor Marcus Aurelius, whose reign lasted from 161 A.D. to 180 A.D, a **plague** spread through Rome's provinces in Europe. Many Romans died and the army was weakened. Rome was no longer conquering rich lands to add money to its treasury. The empire became too large to govern and control. The slow decline of Rome ended in 476 A.D. when Diocletian was **deposed**. The empire was 1,000 years old.

The Romans built cities in the areas they conquered. These columns lined a city street in present-day Jordan, once a Roman province.

Ancient Japan

Ancient Japan was divided into regions, called provinces, each with its own ruler. These local rulers fought each other to control more territory and become more powerful. Over time, the emperors of ancient Japan lost their power to samurai warriors and landholding warlords.

Ruling Clans

Rice farming in Japan was difficult and required many people to work together in the fields. The land was divided into separate regions, each ruled by a group, or clan, of powerful warriors called an *uji*. By 57 A.D., more than 100 *uji* controlled the land that made up Japan. Most people did not belong to an *uji*. Instead, they belonged to families of workers who lived on the land controlled by an *uji*. The working families were organized by the type of work they did into groups called *be*. The members of a *be* had to work hard to produce goods for their *uji*. This earned them the right to live on the land. Each *uji* had several *be*, including a farming, pottery, weaving, and fishing *be*.

Yamato Rule

By 500 A.D., Japan was divided into hundreds of provinces, each ruled by a powerful clan. The most powerful clan was the Yamato on the island of Honshu. Yamato rulers claimed they were descendants of the sun goddess, Amaterasu. Other clans respected the Yamato chieftains for being powerful clan rulers. The Yamato appointed relatives as leaders of clans they conquered and as councilors to supervise peasants' work and collect taxes.

Birth of the Emperor

Other clans fought the Yamato for land. To stop this, the Yamato ruler decided around 600 A.D. that Japan should be ruled by an emperor, like China. Chinese emperors had great power, owned all the land, and were obeyed by the people. In Japan, the emperor or empress was called *tenno*, and was a son or daughter of the previous *tenno*. The *tenno* was treated as a god because he or she was believed to be descended from Amaterasu. Ruling clans kept order over the land even though the emperor owned it.

Organized Government

Some clans rebelled against rule by the emperor. In 645 A.D., Emperor Kotoku chose members of important clans to make up a government and to act as his advisors in running Japan's many provinces. These clan members were rewarded with rice and land for their loyalty to the emperor.

Written Law

Over the next 40 years, the Japanese government produced written laws. Japan's Taiho Code of 701 A.D. and Yoro Code of 718 A.D. stated how crimes should be punished, and how the government should be run. The laws were designed to make people obedient to the emperor. Clan rulers were not allowed to run their former territories. Instead, every 50 houses were grouped together into townships that were run by an overseer. This person supervised the growing of crops and the payment of taxes. People who did not pay their debts were sold into slavery, as were thieves. People who committed violent crimes were executed.

Noble Families

By 858 A.D., the emperor was not as important as he used to be. Noble families had gained much more power and determined how the government was run. Emperors were often children or young adults, and their main function was to perform religious ceremonies. Emperors usually retired early to avoid the boredom of their job.

Prince Shotoku, show with his two sons, wa. an advisor to Empre. Suiko during the Yamato period.

Advisors, who were members of the noble families, carried out the legal responsibilities of the emperor. Nobles constantly fought with each other in order to obtain more influence in the government. Although the emperor was the official ruler, and was supposed to be the highest authority, noble families controlled Japan until 1156 A.D.

The Fearsome Fujiwara

The Fujiwara family, a powerful noble clan, ran Japan's government from 858 A.D. to 1156 A.D. They made their family members regents, which were the most powerful government jobs. The Fujiwara used their authority to obtain land and riches and to get rid of their rivals, often by killing them. Women in the Fujiwara clan were often married to the emperor, who could have many wives. The Fujiwara clan held so much power that it was able to retire an emperor whenever it liked.

The Shogun

The Taira were a samurai clan that controlled Japan from 1160 to 1185. They were poor rulers who ignored the needs of the people. Emperors continued to be religious rulers, but they had no real power. The Taira family made all of the emperor's decisions for him. Around 1180 A.D., a samurai named Minamoto no Yoritomo led a revolt against the Taira clan. This revolt turned into a five-year civil war called the Genpei War. Yoritomo won in 1185 and forced the emperor's government to make him its leader. In 1192, he demanded that the emperor give him the title of *shogun*, meaning "barbarian-suppressing general." This title gave Yoritomo the right to act however he needed to keep peace in Japan. As the *shogun*, Yoritomo had more power than the government and emperor, and became the true ruler of Japan. He then set up a type of government called a *bakufu*, or *shogunate*. The *bakufu* was a military government that controlled the samurai. The emperor and his government of advisors continued to control some of the collection of taxes and the allotment of land to peasants.

Minamoto no Yoritomo

Yoritomo built a new capital at Kamakura on Honshu once he became *shogun*. This was the start of the Kamakura period. Japan was still divided into territories that were run by landholding families. The heads of these families were warlords who paid samurai to protect their land from enemies. The samurai swore loyalty to their lords. In return, they were given land and government positions.

In 1336, a member of a rival clan seized power and became *shogun*. He moved the capital to Kyoto and increased the power of the warlords. The warlords set up armies to keep control over their territories. By 1467 A.D., Japan was divided into dozens of separate territories, with no central control. The War of Onin erupted later that year. It spread through Japan quickly, destroying most of Kyoto. The war ended in 1477, but the warlords, who came to be called *daimyo*, continued to compete with each other to become *shogun*.

Under One Rule at Last

In 1550, a *daimyo* named Oda Nobunaga conquered most of the other *daimyo* and became the *shogun*. He brought almost all of the territories in Japan under his rule before he was killed in 1582. Toyotomi Hideyoshi, the new ruler, completed his work, bringing Japan under one ruler. The emperor continued to perform religious ceremonies at festivals on special occasions.

The child emperor Antoku, above, was attacked by the enemy Minamoto clan in 1185 A.D. Rather than surrender, his grandmother held on to him and jumped into the sea to drown.

Rise of the Samurai

In 794 A.D., the emperor's court was moved to Heian-kyo, or modern-day Kyoto. The court recruited and trained soldiers for an army commanded by nobles. The army maintained law and order and control over the people. Within 200 years, the army's power weakened. People began to acquire weapons to defend themselves instead of relying on the army. The samurai eventually formed and became rich and powerful. They were hired to serve as guards at the emperor's palace, as bodyguards for the nobles or lords, and as police. Samurai practiced fighting skills, including sword fighting, archery, and horseback riding. They believed the greatest act of loyalty to their lord was to die fighting for him. If they lost, were shamed in battle, or if their lord died, samurai killed themselves by slicing their stomachs open. This is called *seppuku*.

The Warrior Code

Samurai obeyed a code of conduct called *bushido*, which stated that courage and pride were more important than anything else. Even when he was outnumbered and defeat was certain, a warrior was never supposed to turn his back on an enemy or try to escape battle. Samurai wore a piece of colored cloth in battle so their acts of bravery could be reported.

1. Samurai began training at the age of five or six. They practiced with wooden swords before they were given a steel sword. Samurai trained for hours, often in physical pain, to develop the strong mind of a warrior. They meditated and fasted, or went for long periods without eating food.

2. Samurai had to be very skilled to shoot bows and arrows, so they practiced all the time. They were famous for being able to shoot a bow and arrow while riding a horse.

3. Bows, first used around 250 A.D., were made of bamboo and were about six feet (two meters) long. Eagle, hawk, or crane feathers were glued to an arrow to make it fly in a straight line. The ancient Japanese invented two types of arrowheads: a four-sided arrowhead that could pierce armor, and a three-pronged arrowhead that could cut rope. A whistle was sometimes attached to the arrow's shaft to signal the attack as it sailed through the air.

4. Swords were more than weapons to the ancient Japanese. They were thought to have powers and lives of their own, their strength and magic affected by the thoughts and actions of the swordsmith. A swordsmith fasted while he worked so he would be pure and the sword he made would be more powerful.

5. Samurai wives had to know how to defend their homes in wartime. They carried a dagger and knew how to fight with a curved sword on a long pole, called a *naginata*.

Ancient Celts

The Celts raided nearby lands for goods and eventually began to settle in the areas they raided, such as present-day France, northern Spain and Italy, Germany, the Balkans, and Bohemia. Celtic communities were made up of clans. A clan was an extended family group that farmed and lived together on a small plot of land. The head of the clan was a king or queen, or an elected chieftain. The constant need to defend their land against invasion by others made the Celts fierce and fearless warriors.

There were at least fifteen different Celtic groups. Historians refer to them together as the Celts because they shared the same original language and way of life. Celts in different areas of Europe had their own chieftains or kings, and groups of Celts often fought each other. The Celts were eventually defeated by the Romans, but some of their descendants still live in western Europe.

Kings, Queens, and Chieftains

There were many rulers at any one time in Celtic lands, as each clan had its own king or queen. To be respected, rulers had to be physically fit, show their wealth, and provide their followers with feasts. Their close relatives made up a class of wealthy nobles. Celtic kings and queens always belonged to the family of the clan's last ruler. In clans ruled by chieftains, the leaders were elected because of their skill in battle and leadership.

Kings and queens held feasts in their homes or outdoors to keep clan members loyal to them. Everyone in the community was invited to attend and eat as much as they wanted. Roasted meats and loaves of bread were served with large amounts of beer and mead, an alcoholic drink made from honey. During the feasts, musicians and poets called bards told tales and songs were sung. Warriors carried out pretend battles to show off their fighting skills.

Kings and queens often owned shields and swords made out of bronze. These were not used in battle, but were brought out during processions and at feasts to show the ruler's wealth. The shields were made of long, thin pieces of bronze, and were attached to wooden backs. Spiral designs were embossed or engraved onto them, and they were studded with pieces of red enamel. Kings also had bronze helmets made for display with plumes of horsehair attached to the top.

Battle Tactics

Celtic battle tactics depended on whom the Celts were fighting. If they were fighting against another Celtic clan, or group, only one man was sent into battle. The chieftains of both clans chose their best warrior to fight in a battle to the death. In battles against other peoples, the Celts lined up facing their enemy. They drank beer or mead, shouted insults at the enemy, sang war songs, and sounded war trumpets to scare the other army. Then, they charged on foot in a row, roaring and screaming. War chariots thundered along beside them. As the chariots reached the battle lines, warriors leaped off and entered the fight.

Druids

Druids were ancient Celtic priests, teachers, and doctors, and were considered the most important people in the community. At least one druid lived in each community. Versed in Celtic histories and knowledge, druids performed religious ceremonies and offered sacrifices to Celtic gods. They also created laws that described how to behave, and acted as judges when someone was accused of a crime.

Warriors

Working men in Celtic communities were expected to go to war when his king or queen commanded it. Celtic warriors stripped naked and often painted their bodies with woad, a blue dye, to frighten their enemies. They carried wooden or wicker shields, sometimes covered with leather. Their weapons consisted of swords and spears, and they fired stones from a leather sling.

The Celts were respected as warriors by other ancient cultures. From 400 B.C. to 300 B.C., they became allies of the ancient Greeks and won three wars with them. Many Celtic warriors joined armies in Syria and Egypt as mercenaries and were paid well for their valuable fighting skills. In 259 B.C., Celtic warriors working for the Egyptian pharaoh, Ptolemy II, rebelled, and tried to establish a Celtic territory in Egypt. They were defeated by the rest of the Egyptian army, and left to starve to death on an island in the Nile River.

Rome is Conquered

The Celts' greatest success in battle was in 387 B.C. Led by a Celtic warrior named Brennus, Celtic raiders from northern Italy met the Roman army a few miles from Rome. The Celts defeated the mighty Roman army in one charge and invaded the city. After burning most of the city to the ground, the Celts besieged the Capitoline Hill, also known as the Capitol, the highest hill in Rome, where the Roman government was located. The defenders stood firm for over six months and the Celts were unable to conquer the hill. The Celts left the city only after the Romans paid them an enormous amount of gold to leave and return to lands farther north. The Romans never forgot their defeat by the Celts, and there was an uneasy peace between the two civilizations for nearly 100 years.

Enemy Neighbors

Celtic groups that had settled new territories across Europe needed to defend the land against invasions by others. The Roman Empire began to expand into central and western Europe around 334 B.C. Around 110 B.C., Germanic groups from northern Europe moved into Celtic territory. The many different Celtic groups were not unified under one leader, making them easier for invaders to conquer. The end of Celtic dominance in Europe arrived when Roman general Julius Caesar conquered most of their lands, beginning around 58 B.C. Celtic ruins can be seen in many European countries today.

Head Hunting

The Celts believed that a person's strength, courage, and wisdom came from their head. The greatest trophy for a Celtic warrior was an enemy's head. The Celts cut off the heads of opponents killed in battle, and tied them to their belts or to the bridles of their chariots' horses. They also suspended the heads from the gateways and ramparts that surrounded their towns. The heads of their most powerful enemies were embalmed in cedar oil in chests, and kept in their homes. Possessing an enemy's head ensured good luck and success, and warded off evil from the fortress or home. Sometimes, Celts placed skulls in food storage pits to protect food from animals, insects, and rot.

A portico of a Celtic stone shrine in France displays human skulls.

Ancient Vikings

From 787 A.D. to about 1000 A.D., Vikings were the world's greatest traders and explorers, and were feared for their deadly raids on other lands. The most powerful people in Viking countries were kings and chieftains, who controlled the land and owned slaves. One of the Vikings' most important developments was their system of government. The Vikings had one of the earliest democratic societies, in which common people, not rulers, made laws.

787 A.D.–1100 A.D.

Kings and Chieftains

Viking kings were powerful leaders who ruled over Scandinavian lands. The lands were divided into territories controlled by chieftains. A Viking became a chieftain through his wealth, his skill in battle, and his ability to command respect from others. The more wealthy a chieftain was, the more followers he attracted. Chieftains increased their power by defeating other chieftains in battles over land.

To keep their followers happy, chieftains held feasts in their halls and served plenty of meat, beer, and mead. Horses were killed as a sacrifice to the Viking gods before being boiled and served to the guests. There was always music, singing, and storytelling at the feasts, and some historians believe the Vikings sometimes wore animal masks during the entertainment.

Thing Meetings

The early Vikings met in outdoor assemblies, known as *things*. There, they settled disputes, passed laws, and judged crimes. Chieftains and land-owning freemen attended *things* to speak, debate, and vote. Men who did not own land, women, and slaves were not allowed to participate, but were sometimes allowed to attend the assembly. Every man attending a *thing* was expected to be peaceful and unarmed.

A victim of a crime or a member of the victim's family attended a *thing* to charge the person suspected of the crime. Twelve *thing* members then tried the accused. Anyone found guilty of a crime had to pay the victim or the victim's family. The amount depended on the seriousness of the crime. A person found guilty who did not pay the fine was banished from the community for a certain length of time.

Things were so important that freemen who owned land were fined if they did not attend.

Murderers were banished for many years and were sometimes never allowed to return. Today, law courts in many countries continue to use the Viking jury tradition. For some types of crime, the accused can choose to be tried by twelve members of a jury made up of members of the local community, rather than by a judge.

Women were not allowed to speak or vote at *things*, even if they owned land. If a woman was accused of a crime, a male family member spoke in her defense. If she was found guilty, her father or husband was held responsible for her actions and had to pay a fine for her punishment.

Iceland's Parliament

In 930 A.D., Iceland created the *Althing*, the world's first parliament. Every summer, Iceland's chieftains met at Thingvellir, where a dip between the mountains made a natural amphitheater. Over a period of two weeks they passed laws and resolved disputes that had not been settled at regional *things*. Every freeman was allowed to speak at Thingvellir if he wished.

The Raiding Season

The Vikings raided in spring and summer, after the crops were planted. To carry out surprise attacks, Viking ships silently approached coasts at dawn. Before the local people had time to gather a defense force, the Vikings landed on the beach and stormed the church or monastery. After stealing treasures, the Vikings sometimes burned the buildings. If it was a long voyage back home, the Vikings raided the nearby towns for food. Anyone who resisted the Vikings was either killed or taken as a slave.

Once on land, Viking warriors stood shoulder to shoulder in rows, advancing against the enemy. Shields were held so that they overlapped and formed a wall that was difficult for the enemy to break. The warriors stabbed at the enemy with short spears and double-edged swords. Some warriors swung heavy iron battle-axes. If a Viking was killed, the shield wall broke down and the Vikings moved into smaller groups to fight. The Vikings despised cowardice and always fought to the end. Their refusal to surrender meant that they sometimes won battles against much larger armies that had archers and cavalry.

The most fearsome Viking warriors were the berserkers. To look more terrifying, they rubbed mixtures of chalk, charcoal, and egg yolk on their faces and wore bearskins into battle to give them the strength of bears. Before battle, berserkers drank a lot of mead and beer, and howled like animals to work themselves into an excited state.

Viking attacks were so ferocious that other countries paid the Vikings to be left alone. The French gave the Vikings part of northern France, known today as Normandy, and paid them 700 pounds of silver every year. When the Vikings conquered most of northern and eastern England in 869 A.D., the territory became known as the Danelaw. The English paid the Vikings with Danegeld, or "tax paid to the Danes," to keep them from attacking farther south.

William the Conqueror

Viking Kings of England

Swein, one of the most fearsome Viking raiders, forced his father, Harald Bluetooth, from the throne of Denmark in 988 A.D. His armies continued to raid the south of England. The young king of England, Ethelred, fled to France. Unchallenged, Swein claimed England's throne in 1014 A.D. England was now under Viking rule. After Swein's death, his son, Canute, took over the thrones of England and Denmark and ruled for the next 20 years.

Succession then fell to Canute's sons, and eventually to Ethelred's son, Edward, who died without an heir. The most powerful man in England was crowned King Harold II. Duke William of Normandy, a relative of King Edward, and King Harald Hardrada of Denmark, a relative of King Canute, both invaded England. Duke William, later known as William the Conqueror, was the victor and was crowned king of England. Norman kings, the descendants of Vikings, now ruled England.

Glossary

administrator A person in charge

alliance A partnership between peoples or countries

ancestor A person from whom one is descended

appointed Chosen for a position

aqueduct A channel for carrying fresh water

assassinate To murder for political reasons

Buddhism A religion founded by Buddha, an ancient religious leader from India

chariot A two-wheeled cart pulled by horses

city-state An independent city, usually walled for defense, and the surrounding towns and villages that depend on it for defense

colonial Describing something from the time when a country was ruled and settled by another country

concubine A mistress or secondary wife

conquistador A Spanish conqueror

deposed Removed from office

despot A ruler with absolute power and authority who often uses that power in a cruel an unfair way; a dictator

dynasty A series of rulers from the same family

empire One political unit that occupies a large region of land and is governed by one ruler

indigenous Native to an area

irrigate To supply land with water through ditches, channels, and canals

Islam A religion that follows the teachings of the prophet Muhammad

meditate The act of thinking quietly

mercenaries Soldiers hired for money to work in the armies of other countries

military expeditions Journeys made by an army for a specific purpose

nomadic Moving from place to place

plague A serious and deadly disease that is often spread to humans by infected fleas and carried by rats

provinces A country or region brought under the control of the Roman government

pyramid Huge structures that usually have a square base and four triangular sides meeting at a point

reliefs Stone carvings in which figures are raised from the background

republic A state or system of government where power rests with citizens who vote for their leaders

revolt To rebel against a government

scholar An expert on one or many things

stucco Plaster used to cover outside walls or decorate inside walls

tribute A payment made by one ruler or nation to another to show obedience or to obtain peace or protection

Index

Websites

www.bbc.co.uk/history/ancient/
    Amazing images highlight in-depth looks into ancient cultures.
www.historyforkids.org/
    This site provides information on the history, food, clothing, technology, stories, and religion of many ancient cultures.
www.pbs.org/wgbh/nova/ancient/
    Interactive videos take readers through ancient civilizations.
www.archaeolink.com/ancient_trade_routes.htm
    Learn about the trade routes between ancient civilizations.

Further Reading

True Books: Ancient Civilizations series, Children's Press 2010

Ancient Warfare series, Gareth Stevens Publishing 2009

Biography from Ancient Civilizations: Legends, Folklore, and Stories of Ancient Worlds series, Mitchell Lane Publishers 2009

Ancient and Medieval People series, Benchmark books 2009

Ancient World Leaders series, Chelsea House Publishing, 2008